# A Teddy Bear for Emily–
## and President Roosevelt, Too

**Nancy Churnin**
illustrated by **Bethany Stancliffe**

Albert Whitman & Company
Chicago, Illinois

With gratitude to my friend Yiddish scholar Miriam Udel for her help,
and my beloved immigrant grandparents, Mary and Samuel Farber, Bessie and Max Churnin,
and bonus grandparents Clara and Bernard Bickel,
who showed thanks for America's welcome by being kind to others.—NC

For Jefferson, Max, and Juliette—BS

Library of Congress Cataloging-in-Publication data is on file with the publisher.
Text copyright © 2025 by Nancy Churnin
Illustrations copyright © 2025 by Albert Whitman & Company
Illustrations by Bethany Stancliffe
First published in the United States of America in 2025 by Albert Whitman & Company
ISBN 978-0-8075-0422-2 (hardcover)
ISBN 978-0-8075-0423-9 (ebook)
All rights reserved. No part of this book may be reproduced or transmitted
in any form or by any means, electronic or mechanical,
including photocopying, recording, or by any information storage and
retrieval system, without permission in writing from the publisher.
Printed in China
10 9 8 7 6 5 4 3 2 1 WKT 30 29 28 27 26 25

Design by Rick DeMonico

For more information about Albert Whitman & Company,
visit our website at www.albertwhitman.com

One minute, Mama and Papa were reading the newspaper.

The next minute, Papa left for their candy shop in Brooklyn, and Mama hurried toward her basket of cloths and buttons with *that look* in her eyes.

Emily swallowed last bites of buttered toast and followed, wondering, *Why is Mama rushing to make a new toy?* But all Emily asked was: "May I help?"

"Yes, *mayn tayere*—my dear. You are nine now, big enough to help." Mama settled baby Benjamin on a blanket. "Can you please hand me the velvet?"

Emily's mouth dropped open. Mama had been saving the velvet since…

"This is special, Mama?"

"Very special, *mayn ziskayt*—my darling. Can you hand me the scissors?"

As Mama snip, snip, snipped, Benjamin fussed. Emily patted him and asked:

"Are we making a cat? A dog? A…"

"Bear!" Mama held two pieces of cloth together. She turned the sides inside out so the velvet sides kissed. Emily had never seen Mama make a bear.

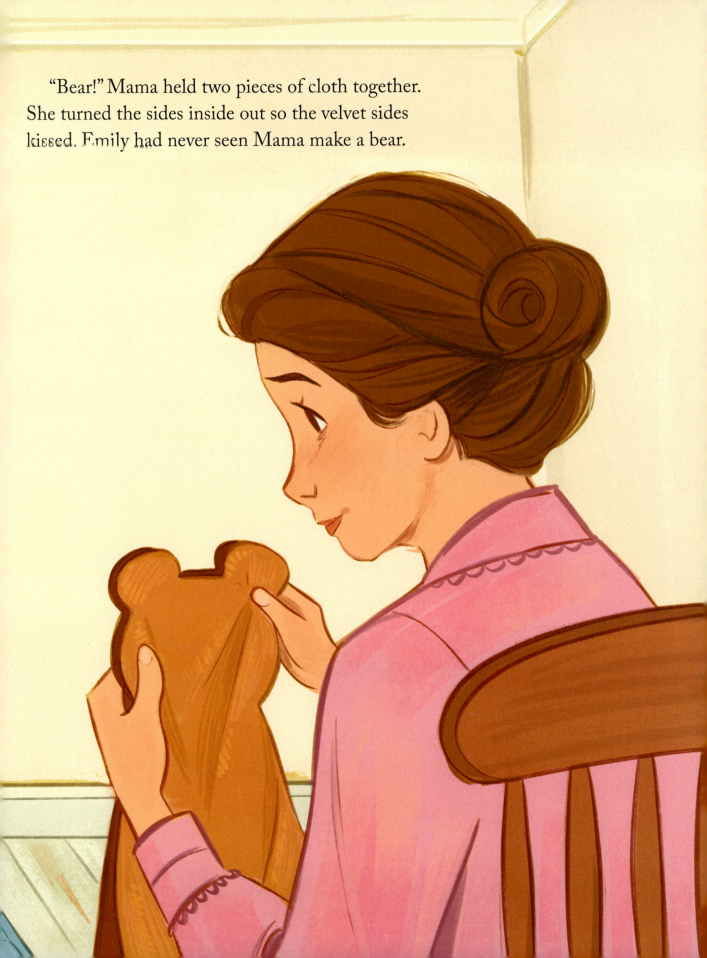

Emily asked, "For Benjamin?" Emily didn't dare ask if it could be for her. But Mama shook her head.

"*Neyn, mayn kind*—no, my child. Can you hand me the needle? The thread?"

Mama's thread flew like a bird through the loop of the needle. She knotted the ends.

"Here," Mama said, handing it to Emily.

This *was* a day of surprises! Mama sang to Benjamin while Emily's needle darted.

"Is it to sell?"

Emily loved seeing Mama's toys peek out among Papa's candies.

"*Neyn, mayn tayere*," Mama said. "It's Teddy's bear."

"Teddy?"

"Our president."

Now Emily was really confused. Why would President Theodore Roosevelt want a toy bear?

"Let me tell you a story."

Mama wrapped the sleeping Benjamin in his blanket and drew close as Emily stitched.

"Once, long before you were born, a boy with a big heart got on a boat to America. Morris…"

Emily interrupted: "My papa?"

"Yes, *dayn tateh*—your papa. He was a few years older than you are now. His parents were sad. But they knew that Jewish people in Russia weren't safe in 1887. They hoped he'd find kindness in America."

Mama nodded approvingly at Emily's stitches.

"On the boat, Morris clutched a toy his mother had sewn for him when he was small. A child with sad eyes looked at him. Morris hesitated, then handed his toy to her. She offered it back, but he shook his head. The girl's smile lit his heart."

*That's so like my papa!*

"When Morris arrived in America, he had less than when he'd stepped on the boat. But he felt as if he had more. Because he knew he'd find kindness by being kind."

Mama knotted threads. Emily trimmed them.

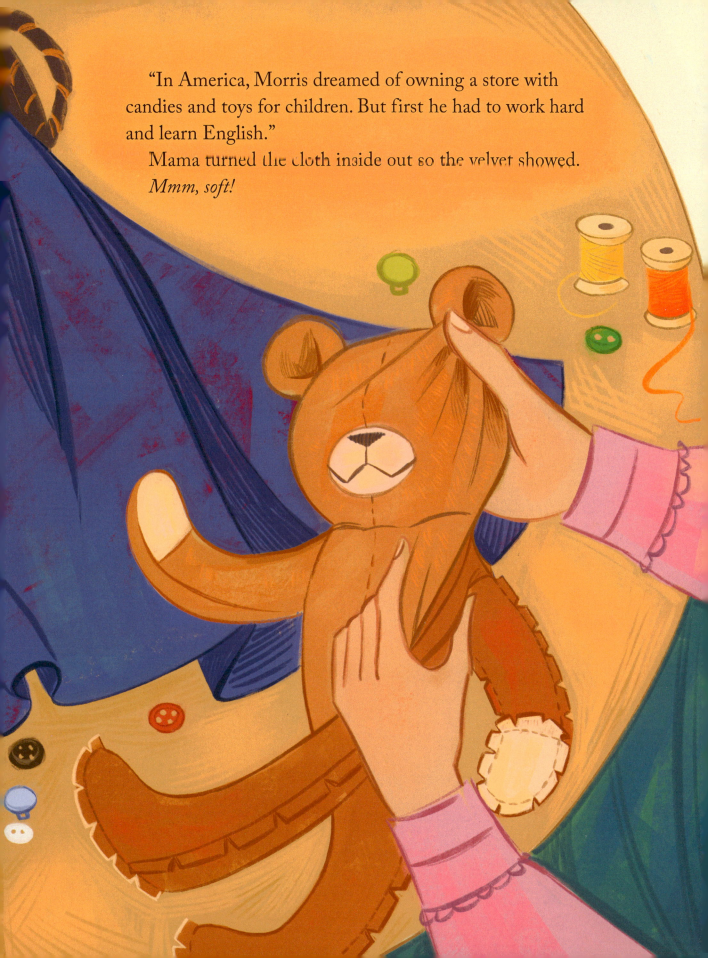

"In America, Morris dreamed of owning a store with candies and toys for children. But first he had to work hard and learn English."

Mama turned the cloth inside out so the velvet showed. *Mmm, soft!*

"Coin by coin, dollar by dollar, Morris saved enough to buy a shop at 404 Tompkins Avenue. Then, *drrring*! Rose Katz walked in, looking for work.

"'*Gut morgn*—good morning,' she said."

"That was you, Mama!"

Mama nodded, face glowing.

Emily helped Mama stuff the bear. *I wonder if it tickles!*

"Rose told Morris she, too, had fled danger in Russia. She shared how she wanted to work at the candy shop, bringing joy to children. Morris told her about his dream to make toys. He showed her cloths and sketches.

'I have ideas, but not skills,' he told her.

'*Ikh ken zey makhn*—I could make those,' she murmured."

"You did, Mama!"

Mama stitched the plump bear closed.

"Your Papa and I married. We spent our honeymoon in our shop. Papa sketched. I brought his drawings to life with needle and thread. We had sweet children—including Emily…"

"Me! And Benjamin."

Mama sewed a button on the bear's face.

*Is he winking at me?*

"Then *this* happened." Mama pushed the newspaper toward Emily. Emily read that the president, who used to hunt wild animals, had spared a bear's life. *Another act of kindness*, she thought.

Mama handed Emily the finished bear. Emily hugged it. She felt the love they'd sewn into it as she skipped alongside Mama to their store.

Proudly, Papa put the bear in the window under the sign: "Teddy's Bear."

*Drrring! Drrring! Drrring!*
"How much is Teddy's Bear?"
"It's not for sale," Emily's papa said.
*Drrring! Drrring! Drrring! Drrring! Drrring! Drrring!*
More people wanted to buy Teddy's Bear. Papa said no again and again.

"Emily, I don't know if the president wants us selling a bear with his name…"

Emily could see Papa was worried. What was it her parents had told her to do when she didn't know the answer?

"Papa, why don't you ask him?"

Papa looked startled. Then he grinned.

"Of course, *mayn* Emily!"

In 1902, there wasn't a quick way to get a message from New York City to the White House in Washington, DC. The United States Postal Service used horse-drawn wagons. Papa packed the bear with a note, offering it as a gift. Emily hoped the president's children would love the bear as much as she did and understand that Emily's family was thanking the president in their language—the language of toys.

Still, she worried. Would this powerful person read a request from a poor family in Brooklyn? As the horses clop, clop, clopped, Emily and her parents waited…
 and waited…
  and waited…

Finally, a letter arrived. Emily's parents let her open it. Slowly, she read…

*Yes!* President Roosevelt didn't see how his name would help the bear, but they could use it.

The president knew about running the country, but Emily's family knew what made kids happy. Mama sewed bears for Emily and Benjamin and many, many children. Emily helped!

Soon, everywhere they looked, kids—including President Roosevelt's children!—were cuddling, comforting, and comforted by what they now called teddy bears.

Emily was proud that her family was bringing kindness to so many children.

By 1904, an equally proud President Roosevelt began showing teddy bears at White House events. In 1917, thirty years after Morris had arrived in New York as a hopeful teenager, he and Rose shuttered their candy shop to follow their *new* dream: making teddy bears to brighten hearts all over the world.

# Author's Note

On the surface, people couldn't seem more different than a poor Jewish immigrant couple like Morris and Rose Michtom and the powerful president of the US, Theodore Roosevelt. But one of the most beloved and comforting of all toys, the teddy bear, might never have been born without the connection between them.

Although that connection might seem unlikely or surprising, it is a reminder of how much we all have in common, whether we work in a little Brooklyn candy shop or in the White House—the name that Theodore Roosevelt gave to the president's home.

President Roosevelt had already been admired by the Michtoms for his support of immigrants when he was governor of New York from 1899 to 1900. Their appreciation of him grew when he sent a message to the country by sparing a bear in Mississippi on November 14, 1902—a message of kindness and mercy. As soon as children saw the bear the Michtoms had made, it reminded them of what the president had done. It made them want to cuddle and be kind to it. And that's when the magic happens. Because when we cuddle and care for our teddy bears, it makes us feel cuddled and cared about, and connected to others who love their toys, too. The president's children loved Teddy's Bear as much as the Michtom children and all the children who clamored for their own bears did.

There is no evidence that the Michtoms' daughter, Emily, helped sew that first Teddy's Bear in 1902. But she would have been nine at the time—a good age to help and learn why her parents were honoring the president in this way.

Years later, Emily's husband, David Rosenstein, would become an executive with her parents' toy company, and her baby brother Benjamin was named co-chairman.

The Michtoms called the first bear Teddy's Bear, after the president, affectionately known to Americans as Teddy. While proof of the letter they sent to the president asking his permission to use his name doesn't exist, they always claimed that they didn't sell it until they requested and received permission from the president to call it Teddy's Bear—a name that was later shortened to "teddy bear."

No one had exclusive rights to creating stuffed bears. Richard Steiff designed a toy bear around the same time in 1902 in Germany that was displayed in 1903, the same year that Rose and Morris founded their Ideal Novelty & Toy Company.

Many famous stuffed bears followed: Winnie-the-Pooh, or Pooh Bear (based on a teddy bear owned by A.A. Milne's son, Christopher Robin, who became the hero of the Pooh books), Paddington Bear (based on the hero of the Michael Bond book series), Corduroy Bear (which debuted as a toy, followed by a series of books), Care Bears (which launched as greeting card images), Teddy Ruxpin (a best-selling toy), and Build-a-Bear.

One thing all these bears have in common is that these soft, cuddly, huggable toys have brought joy to children. And if you're wondering what happened to the original Teddy's Bear that the Michtoms placed in their shop window with such pride and care, you'll find it at the Smithsonian Museum of American History in Washington, DC, where it was donated by grandchildren of the original "Teddy"—President Theodore Roosevelt.

"…if the immigrant who comes here in good faith becomes an American and assimilates himself to us, he shall be treated on an exact equality with everyone else, for it is an outrage to discriminate against any such man because of creed, or birthplace, or origin."

—President Theodore Roosevelt